G000079627

In The Ninth House

LOUISE C. CALLAGHAN

salmonpoetry

Published in 2010 by
Salmon Poetry
Cliffs of Moher, County Clare, Ireland
Website: www.salmonpoetry.com
Email: info@salmonpoetry.com

Copyright © Louise C. Callaghan, 2010

ISBN 978-1-907056-52-9

All rights reserved. No part of this publication may be reproduced or transmitted in
any form or by any means, electronic or mechanical, including photography,
recording, or any information storage or retrieval system, without permission in
writing from the publisher. The book is sold subject to the condition that it shall not,
by way of trade or otherwise, be lent, resold or otherwise circulated without the
publisher's prior consent in any form of binding or cover other than that in which it is
published and without a similar condition, including this condition, being imposed on
the subsequent purchaser.

Cover artwork: "Liath" by Sarah McEvoy. Fused, cut and polished glass.
Image reproduced with the kind permission of the artist.
www.sarahmcevoyglass.com
Cover design & typesetting: *Siobhán Hutson*
Printed in England by imprint*digital*.net

Salmon Poetry receives financial assistance from the Arts Council

For my much loved sister Gaye

Acknowledgements

Acknowledgement and thanks to the editors who first published the following poems:

Poetry Ireland Review Issue 94, 2008: "Dynamo"
The Irish Times April 2nd, 2009: "Egg Money"
Copenhagen Review (online), November 2008: "Pallas Athena"
The Red Wheelbarrow 2006, 2007: "Fragments" and "At St. Andrews"
Salmon: A Journey in Poetry, 1981-2007 (Salmon Poetry, 2007): "Grandma's Summer Cottage"
Thornfield: Poems by the Thornfield Poets (Salmon Poetry, 2008): "Only Goya", "Grandma's Summer Cottage"
The Living Streets: Anthology of the Ranelagh Arts Festival (The Seven Towers, 2009): "Musée du Moyen Âge Tapestries", "In a Garden of Birds", "For the Baby in the Wet Suit"

"The Binder's Notes", shortlisted for the Strokestown International Poetry Prize, 2009.

Thanks to the staff of the Tyrone Guthrie Centre, Annaghmakerrig, the Centre Culturel Irlandais, Paris, and to the Committee of the Strokestown International Poetry Festival.

Thanks to Thornfield Poets and WEB.

A special thanks to Susan Connolly and Maggie O'Dwyer for their friendship and support over many years and to Gaye C. Polacsek and Ruth Barry for their abiding interest in my work.

Contents

Waiting for Frogs to Hop

Two-and-a-Half   11
Getting Out by Myself   12
Heron   13
For the Baby in the Wet Suit   14
Reading & Writing   15
The Trick Is...   16
Making & Doing i, ii, iii   17
Jubilee   20
In a Garden of Birds   22
Traders Magneto Dynamo Company   23
Longer Days   24
Fledged   25
Every September   26
Growing Up   27
'If I were a blackbird'...   28
Egg-Money   29
Ballad of the Little Tailor of Dunino   30
Musée du Moyen Âge Tapestries   33
Longing for Fame   34
Waiting for Frogs to Hop   35

In the Ninth House

Fragments   39
Athena in Mourning   41
Pallas Athena   43
Winter in Inis Meáin   44
Immram: Inis Meáin   47
Homeguard Earlies   57
November Ghost   59
Death of a Dog   61
The Summer Cottage   62

Getting Started Again

An Artist & His Letters - 4 Poems   69
Release Scheme, Bhutan   73
The Marriage Gift   74
Trapping the Unicorn   75
Only Goya   76
Netta M. Mitchel   79
After the Wedding   80
Conference of Frogs   81
Poets & Frogs   82
Halcyon-Bird   83
At St. Andrews   84
The Binder's Notes   85
Colophon   87
Dynamo   88
Annaghmakerrig Revisited   89

A Note About the Ninth House   91

About the Author   93

Waiting for Frogs to Hop

Two-and-a-Half

Once again I lift the plaid cloth to peep
into the dark space under the table,
to see their baby among stockingless legs
and broken-down shoes – her bare bottom.

Then next-door, up and down the empty room
shoving before me a red tin hen, its sharp
clackety-clack wings and whining wheels
I scuttle over the splintered boards.

And I've found the baby's bed, the small nest
in the lower drawer of their bedroom chest,
for this is 1950 – off Fitzwilliam Square:
lamplit rooms over the coachhouse stable.

If you'd peered in that window under the roof
you'd have seen Lally at the table, her sister May,
Jimmy and the old father with the iron hook
screwed into the end of his wooden arm.

Getting Out by Myself

But perhaps my earliest
is a memory of balancing
over the crossbar of my cot,
that moment – teetering

between two worlds –
a rotund torso, one leg up,
perilous drop as over you go
onto liver-coloured lino.

Heron

I saw a heron once standing here
on the slant-glass of the summer house,
a silvery-grey figure I always intended
to picture in a poem. That's when you
were just a yearning in your parents' eyes.

And now here you are at my window
with a miniaturist's eye, and small finger
smudging the inside glass: *yes, birdies* –
I supply the words – for the birds,
unmistakably, far away up in the sky.

For the Baby in the Wet-Suit

(Anna Scout Barry)

The frogs were stacked
one on top of another
on the surface of the pond.

From here their croak,
more a purr. Overnight
a mass of spawn formed

on the brimming water.
Each jellied cell
held a curled-up dot.

I watched the tadpoles
unfold – flicker and turn
all through her first Summer.

The ragged sacks,
a dirty milk-colour,
like a lucky birth-caul.

Reading & Writing

I still see the shallow balsaboard drawers
stacked in rows by the classroom door.
And still feel that dry disagreeable pull
of a drawer without runners. At eye-level,
your own one, unresinous, wafer-thin,
with its own name-label. There for you
to place cards of sandpaper letters in,
(braille-trace it – with your finger)
and the sheets of your shape-drawings
and the blameless first reader. In a trance
you stand before the narrow drawer, all
your attempts at reading, ended in despair.

The Trick Is...

Leaning over that first reader,
eyes fixed to your finger,
you try to configure a flow
out of the alphabet-words

till called by the bell for *break*
to return your own little book
to its shallow cabinet drawer.
The trick is not to let anyone

see the wet-stain on the back
of your school skirt.
You remain on in the squat chair,
but really you disappear.

Making & Doing

i

A blackbird mimics raindrops on the lawn:
bird's-foot drumming over and back...
Snowflakes fall on the grass, covering in
the skylight. You, Oscar and I iglood inside.

ii

You drew a dog, a small greyhound centred
on your bare A5 page. Oscar drew monsters,
flying, swimming, some grinning wistfully.
That boy loves to scare, *himself* more than us.

iii

The afternoon was threaded through with
muffled bird-song. It snowed and snowed.
You showed me how to *image* on my laptop:
Theseus, the hero and the hairy half-man monster.

Jubilee

for Cillian

What a wonderful bird the frog are...
         Anon

From mid-night to one,
at the kitchen window

I watch six frogs
on the apron

of the garden lawn.
They're oblivious to

props of wrought-iron
furniture: a table

and two chairs,
my garden seat.

Unphased by the heat-
sensitive light

I reset inside
every few minutes,

unaware of my stare,
they sit upon rear ends

waiting for a slug
to come along

or a centipede.
Indoors in the dark

I'm transfixed by one
throat pulsing

to the rhythm
of rainbeat on grass

masking the intent
of an amphibious heart.

In a Garden of Birds

for little A.B

Imagine if birds could talk, the pigeon
in its roomy plumage homing-in
on my lawn would be the loudest –
like those native speakers on the Luas,
how they bludgeon us with their blas –
Budge over it would say, *I got here first.*
Birds fly in all day, dropping down like

break-away leaves from the dying lilac,
the smallest slip through the cross-hatch trellis,
then from fuchsia to fence-post hang
suspended from three feeders. A dozen
or so sparrows, coal-tits and goldfinches
enliven our desultory afternoons then
just as suddenly go. A thrush on the bough

motionless as a fisherman, mountain-ash
berries reflected on its chest and best
loved the little wren who shadows
the garden wall. Though all are welcome,
even viking-droves of starlings. Magpies,
in two's please. Oh and the dear robin
to the dead-of-night song of a blackbird.

Traders Magneto Dynamo Company

TMDC started our father's day
much the same way
as AMDG headed ours:
those careful pencil-letters
in the lefthand margin
at the top of our school copies,
day and date opposite that.
Everything that we wrote
was devoted to God.

Father aspired to motorcars
and the manufacture
of small car parts. But first
he'd drive us to school
in his lovely old 50s Rover
with wide running-boards.
The bell that brought order
to our lives ringing out as
I'd climb from the back seat.

Longer Days

The O in the nesting-box
is a yes, an invitation
to nest. All February
to April, blue-tits
dip into the dark
carrying bits of moss,
straw, a silver-grey feather.
Then there are days,
hours, my eyes water
watching for signs.
Heart-lift as the
entry is crossed again.

Fledged

for Lara Páircéir

A busy pair to and fro
with beaked bits
for their summer young.
Then each small bird
in turn, fills the O
of the nesting-box.

For the first time
out comes one
onto a nearby fence –
strange parental hiss
when one flies down
too close to the ground.

I hold myself tense,
count, a tally of five.
All that time
I'd yearned to eye
inside the dark hive.
Little blue-bonnets

balancing, now flown,
gone with the old moon.

Every September

The reddy-brown sheet came away with me
the day I went to boarding school.
Laid out on the mattress of the little bed,
its dreadful smell, its heaviness. Leaden
as the bib you wear in the raised chair
when dentist and nurse both retreat
behind their safe door, so you alone
receive the flash unclothing bone.
All the ruined mattresses... Oh, but now
let me revel in Septembers – at home!

Growing Up

Facing its womanly girth first I'd search
under frills of leaf for a branch to grip
then purchase for a foot to lever myself up.

By then each sister had claimed her own
quarters in the deciduous torso: one of four
slope-trunks reaching out of its central bole.

Another grip, a niche and I'd be up level
with the vestibule – leaning out over
Chestnut's rough bark, poised to enter

my private world. But however I tried
that dense foliage, however heartset,
the last foothold was still too high.

'If I were a blackbird...'

On the garden wall
a brown blackbird
crouches at dawn.

In this melancholy light
it hops the lines
of frosted furrows

searching for grubs,
particular insects.
As light begins

to brighten
it slips into the pages
of my notebook.

Egg-Money

for Amanda

Never a hen was born, she'd say
that didn't die in debt…
But you were her first care.

In the loft then herself and Jimmy
lived with their daughters
and Billy when he came along.

Under the arch to the rear
of the Square, the cobbled yard
where she raised chickens.

And now *you* always say:
'she was the heartbeat of the city'.

Ballad of the Little Tailor of Dunino

for Nuala Watt

Not someone we'll forget,
the little tailor —
walking these old coal-roads
from place to place

no more than a canvas bag
strapped to his back
with scissors & measuring rod.
From Boarhill he'd come

through Dunino Woods
whistling like a blackbird
By the hollow in the dell,
over the rickety bridge

and before morning mist
lifted he'd be here
under our windows,
his call at the open door.

Nothing is left
but the headstone,
not a word, nor date

to stitch his life together,
to say how once
upon a time...

Only a scissors
incised into grey
locally quarried stone,

a skull & crossbones
and an hourglass
remember him.

No-one will know
how he passed
these sunken lanes,

hurrying along
dank mud-paths
through the woods

brushing nettles
and lowered heads
of cowparsley

or trumpet-bindweed,
dead by nightfall.
How in Spring,

one much like this,
sniffing hazel-blossom
oil-scented air

he'd hurried on,
eager to pass
the shady Den.

Was he frightened then
the stories we've
heard were true?

Musée du Moyen Âge Tapestries

Touchez avec les yieux mes enfants
their teacher reasoned – some
of his students still so young
they may understand only
the language of touch.

And there's always one girl
who reaches her hand out
to a little beast, a rabbit perhaps
crouched in the blue-stitch grass,
or tries to pick a seasonless

millefleur, an ox-eye daisy,
scabious or lady's bedstraw,
recalling the girl-child who caused
her mother to search for her
through all the saddened Earth.

Longing for Fame

I copied his *Cypresses*
and entered it
in a painting competition
for children, the Caltex.

I yearned to recreate
the texture of his
struggling
sinuous trees

those outermost branches
where they meet
the short strokes
of midnight-blue sky

(outside the asylum)*

colour-wheel
of the dizzying
summer sun.
But what if I had won?

NOTE: The asylum at St-Remy where Vincent
Van Gogh, suffering from epilepsia and periodic
attacks of manic depression, voluntarily committed
himself.

Waiting for Frogs to Hop

Raindrops sparkle
where the light
catches them.
Startle when they fall

onto wet leaves
among silver sheaths
of white iris,
among the fleur-de-lys.

In the Ninth House

.

Fragments

for Felicity Yates

Sung at weddings,
sung again
at birthday festivities.

Recited by Cleis
her daughter
under the almond trees.

Memorized, copied out,
countless times
translated.

Read by us
here last night
at your kitchen table:

Aeolian songs
on papyrus,
which for years were

torn into strips,
used to wrap
bodies of the dead.

★

In winter sunshine
we scoured the hills
behind your house

for rock-mementoes.
Sappho of Lesbos,
of Scala Eressos

walked these hills
with her scholar-girls.
Feathered shoots of dill

and the same slow sea.
What troubled her
now troubles me.

Athena in Mourning

1.

After they'd agreed to meet
at Olympic Airways agency
on main Syntagma Square

he set off to find the figurine
he'd only ever seen before
in his Classic's textbook

up jasmine-scented side streets,
well shaded from the sun.
I don't know what she did

all afternoon in that heat
except wait for him to come back.
I see her standing outside

the plate-glass window,
traffic roaring all around.
When they did meet – hours late

I know he took the blame.
There were two offices the same
on opposite sides of the Square.

2.

Shaken about in a *Blue Line* bus
they raced on towards Delphi –

omphalos of the ancient world.
But the girl's morning-sickness

forced the driver to pull over,
let her down to vomit in the dust.

Skirting the base of Mt. Parnassus,
the gods showed not the least interest

in their mortal concerns counting dates
back and forth from her last

menstrual blood. And back home,
the shame when it became known

that their wedding had been shot-gun.

Pallas Athena

The goddess threw her warring
            spear aside,
            and her shield...

It seems to me
            three decades later
            and more

the sad arc of her helmet
            is bowed for
            some mortal loss:

that gentle-eyed Pallas
            was the psalm
            of her saddness.

With love's arms around her
            they wrestled and played,
            girl and goddess,

tasselled wings mingled
            with lustrous
            oil-dark hair,

how perfectly
            they matched.
        I can hear them laugh.

But too easily she snapped.
            In pity and sorrow,
            Athena took her name.

Winter in Inis Meáin

*

A harebell, blue as the sea,
in a bitter wind, anchored deep,
like the Muire-blue shining out
from Harry Clarke's chapel window.

★

When the sun rises, tall skies
are mirrored in rain puddles.
On our walk to the airstrip, lights
blossoming in the factory.

*

At dawn, a swan
leading swan-brothers
towards the Atlantic:
their synchronic wing-beat.

Immram: Inis Meáin

The immensity of sky,
its murmuring reflection
in flagstone rock-pools.

No verticals to speak of,
only poles holding power-lines,
an occasional person

moving on the horizon.
The whole day
talks to me from the sky.

The two brothers
work their long-handled forks
conjuring spuds from the lazybeds.

These are stored away
in *Black Diamond* sacks,
stalks left to rot in a battered creel.

Cows crop quietly around his door:
soft hooves, coughing breath
for company. Concertinas of smoke
find the gap in the ruined thatch.

Our ferry shines through the surf
from its berth in Inis Oirr:
tractors, vans and salt-coroded cars
all converge on the pier.

At the stern with the Filipino women
we are out-numbered by the men.
The same men who searched

three weeks ago for John Dirrane,
recovered only to be buried. From here
we watch the islands disappear.

She is the one who assists at a birth,
helps aunt or sister having her baby.
Cramp-cries, neither English nor Irish.

She'll be first to see the bloodied crown,
to cup the wet head, the fleece of hair.
She who will declare the baby's gender.

Cinn Abhaile, almost a village,
a last gathering of houses
on the furtherest headland,

hill-sheltered from the worst
the Atlantic might hurl.
These past nights draped

by the northern Borealis:
purples, reds, and
the strangest lime green.

At the Pier I said goodbye to a friend
then continued over to the New Cemetery
to pay my respects to the dead.

One headstone read: *Paidín Maolciaráin*,
age, 82. Another, a brother of Dara Beag.
"Greetings: God be with you," I said.

To-day outdoor Mass was celebrated
in the burial ground below the ancient Fort.

Following earlier pagan ways
I trampled the old year underfoot:

eggshell of egg missiles flung at us
last night by sheeted ghosts, by ghouls.

Nobody goes around
the back of the island.
No one builds here.

The loneliness, the keening
of the sea reminds me
of my girl-self

being sent to Coventry,
my death wish
in the suck of the tide.

I wanted to say something that
wouldn't wash away the next day,
catch the music of the waves –

spray clawing the air as it fell back.
I have watched, listened with Winter,
bitten into silence. Said what I can.

Homeguard Earlies

Whether they flower or not
if there's to be no further growth

then I should lift the tubers, snout
them out with a spade or trowel.

The green above ground, past its best
leaf-edge blighted, so I begin to dig

loosen then pull at the wilted stalks.
How easily they come, as my first birth

after a day's hard work in labour.
A dozen or so potatoes hanging off

shrivelled cords like baubles
on left-out Christmas trees, or think

of the *moly*, Homer's lucky charm
against hunger and misfortune

on your journey. Crouching down
I delve my hands into rich dark soil,

entrance among flitters of an old
fireworks display and bits of eggshell

to find more, like dappled stars,
luminous planets revolving in the

Ninth House of one's natal chart.
Bunched in a dish they smell of clay,

of frost March mornings, of life...
survival. Overhead, two magpies

squabble in the canopy of tree-foliage
dinning the *aves* of an Angelus bell.

And I tell myself – it's alright,
alright in a body no longer young.

November Ghost

To end all…in sea-freeze,
on the edge of a moor –
last pitch into darkness.
Found scattered over miles.

You were no more
than a remembered habit,
a feature in some child's face.
Then after years, this dream.

★

It is your skin, yes
and your hazel eyes. Alive
you were forever pinching
the tip of your nose
or gulping air out of
your cupped palm.
Here you are now urging
or is it asking me to dance!

★

As couples we passed once
by the circle of Fates,
Stephen's Green. She followed
behind you with a mongrel dog
tied to a piece of string.
The next time we four meet,
she and I have bumps pushing out
under our woolen jumpers.

★

And I remember one November
dusk, watching from my car
as a thousand rooks settled
into black leafless trees –
not far from where your remains
lie buried. In the grave
between two yews, views
across fields to Curtlestown.

Death of a Dog

for Gail Polacsek

He stands for hours on end you said;
those pool-black eyes focussed on one
table leg or wonders in the persian rug,
as though minding some secret. Or
maybe sensing that void in the hour
we children used to call angels passing.
You only who hear the uneven heartbeat.

He turned aside from your minced liver,
or the warmed-up milk, I suggested –
instead he went outside to the *Weisenau*
and answering a deeper law, drank snow-
water from a puddle in your back yard.
Isn't this how we should die too,
stop eating – stare down the future?

The Summer Cottage

for Tulla Juvonen

No niin, hey-hey / So long, bye-bye

perfect
In the summer cottage we raised
mosquito nets over each narrow bed
as a bride hangs her wedding dress.
The air, you said, sweet as birds' milk.
We woke to lake-water lapping
and light flickering on the window sill
to see where we have slept –
under branches of antlers mounted
on the wall. A silent cuckoo-clock.

pluperfect
Everything on the walls is old or discarded,
a series of still-lives: the glossy head-bone
of an antlered moose – bark-licking tongue,
long gone – the clock prompted to start again,
its laquered bird inside jacks out the hours
and half hours, one pine cone on weight-chains
droops deeper and deeper. The sun never sets
this side of mid-night. A hunter's horn strap-hung
on uprise-antennae, a green hunting jacket.

present
You tie a switch of birch branches
to bring in the steam-house cabin.
We whip arms and legs and buttocks
as leaves release their pungent scent.
Ahead of me I see you flit between
trees, a naiad, then diving in the lake.
Nights like these we eat lightly
then massage each other's feet.

imperfect

Prepared once more for the ceremony
of sleep, I notice the night inside
is darker than the night outside.
Then, your breath-light snores
and a lake-sibilance at the shore
where rounded rocks earlier
seemed just like seal-visitors.
Your poor Grandma trapped indoors
in Kuhmo, the apartment stairs
prevent her coming down. Out here
on the verandah the lake is blueberry,
the sun, lighting towers of cloud.

future
When I was leaving Grandma invited me
back again: You must stay, she said
with Tuula, out at the summer cottage.
She held my hands, aged with rust stains,
her own hands, locked and twisted.
Eyes that had witnessed the Winter War.
But I will not be here then, she said, next year.
You translate all this for her from Finnish.

i.m Aili Mater,
d. 2006

Getting Started Again

An Artist & His Letters – 4 Poems

Getting Started Again

In his *Still Life With Plate of Onions*, a pipe
sits on the table next to a letter from Theo
and a homeopathy handbook: Raspail's
'Annuaire de la Santé'. Extreme anxiety
I'd say, caused Vincent to write: *Light
a candle, make a pot of tea, this is how
I'm going to get started.* Tomorrow, you'll see.

Two Portraits

I tried to paint his empty place:
the Yellow House, Gauguin fled.

He copied the more ornate of two chairs
after the friendship foundered.

On its surface, two books
and a lit candle in a candle-stick.

Here in the museum, the portrait
of it and his own rough chair,

a plain unpainted súgán. The clay pipe
recurs. Battling my claustrophobia

I try to get closer with my notebook.
One chair outstares the other.

Man Pulling a Harrow

In his letter-sketch to Theo, he spoke of
the determination required to be an artist:
One must take it up with assurance, he wrote
*with a conviction… Like the peasant guiding
his plough, or, like our friend, harrowing.*

Or the unfortunates in his watercolour,
Bleaching Ground At Scheveningen –
white dots, confidently dutch-bonnets
and sheets under-billowing on the Green.
The barren foreground, a desolate scene.

What appeals most though is that he believed
his duty was to put his feelings in his work:
loneliness, isolation. But his brush must
have awakened joy also: *Plains of Auver*,
even as he despaired, a miracle of creation.

Landscape, July 1890

I feel a failure he wrote
from Auvers where
he was alone again.

But ever seeking
to console with colour,
his broken brush-stroke

painted crows rising
out of wheatfields,
(startled by gun-shot?)

the wheels of indigo
over cobalt –
his stunned sun

and the red track
through fields of seething
yellow harvest,

the fields where he'd
angled the shotgun
into his own depth.

Release Scheme, Bhutan

Curled in a pail
speckled golden-green

three trout
gulping their silence.

Long prayer-flags
flapping

in the breeze
a highland blessing.

On the skyline
another prisoner

climbs to where
the loch opens

its heart to the sky.
Poured in

new trout-stock
will buy his freedom.

The Marriage Gift

for Biene & Roland

The little pear tree cut right through,
lies on their new-mown meadow grass:
the frayed yellow of an unmendable wound.

But for that star last night falling
from end-of-summer skies we'd be hopeless.
All eyes, I'd panned the bellied dome

when in one brief swoop, it fell clear of time.
I wished my wish, certain of its fulfilment
as you are reading our charts' *north-nodes*

or scenting cyclamen at the edge of the woods.
O happy star I thought, not far, not far,
like a dream waiting to be retrieved.

Trapping the Unicorn

After a break the women resume
their seats on the bench. Shoulder
touching shoulder they lean in
to the strap-frame of the loom –
not bending over saves your back.
From the ground they work up

weft following as you'd read a book
from left to right. The warp, like
strands of grass ripening in a field.
Lifting threads left off an hour ago
they connect one shade to another,
building the story with colour:

samite and rose and that particular
shade of green shown in the cartoon,
interwoven with golden threads.
Two hunters' heads emerge. And so
the scene grows, slowly, slowly
between the woman-weavers' knees.

Only Goya

The White Duchess

Linked by legend and rumour,
Maria del Pilar, Duchess of Alba:

the most beautiful woman in all
Spain. Her black ringlet-curls,

silk undercurrant of her skirts,
out-turn of her tiny slippered feet.

Notebook Drawings

His notebooks are full of drawings
of life at Doñana, her country estate.

He sketched portraits of her,
her and her entourage in pen and ink.

Old Trinidad, and Catalina
her maid, the idiot Benito

and Amor the dwarf.
The little black child they called

Mari-Luz, cradled in her lap.
His fantasies are hiding here too,

her naked among the bedclothes.
Her laughter entered his silent world

The Black Duchess

She is standing on the shore
of a murky yellow estuary –

(the quicksand of his happiness?).
He has signed *Sólo Goya*

marked it with a stick in the sand
at the tip of her ballerina feet.

She points to this as if
to question a butterfly-kiss.

You wonder if he knew his
signature was soon to be erased,

hidden for years
under a layer of brown ochre?

Netta M. Mitchel

d. April 1964

Mother speaks to the bones
as she crosses over
each bed-size space

to leaf-strewn paths
dividing plot from plot,
mutters apologies.

In a hat — she says
Irene Gilbert made
whenever it's admired

of crocheted
forget-me-nots, and
her fur-lined boots

she plods up and down.
*The lay of the graves
has changed,* she claims

since the last time
she came looking for
her dear one, her mother.

After the Wedding

Clots of apple-blossom
are falling already
from this old appletree

fluttering-down petals
of confetti, scattered
easter-snow in May.

But if, as we've heard,
it is not attended
by the pollinating bees,

then there must surely
be a sense of futile
accomplishment.

Conference of Frogs

The frogs reposition themselves
at the outer edges
of the heat-seeking light
thrown onto our curtilage of lawn.

When the latest news announces
force winds and flood water;
bomb-blasts from whatever war is
currently being fought,

frogs are our warning beacons,
an unlikely chorus in the rain,
whose torrents are beating down
curses on the princes of oil.

Poets & Frogs

In Aristophanes' *The Frogs*,
Dionysus complains there are no
decent playwrights left. He
proposes a trip to the underworld
for a contest between the dead
masters of Comedy. But first,
before leaving he asks Hericles
for the fastest route to Hades,
whereupon the wit replies, suicide
should bring him there in no time.

In the original *Frogs*, frogs merely
supply the chorus. Added to that
insult they sing off stage: *ko-ax*,
ko-ax, ko-ax. In the musical
on Broadway, Sondheim's frogs
are more incidental to the plot. Not
even chorus–girls in flared skirts,
they perch upon cocktail glasses in
programme notes & publicity material.

Halcyon-Bird

Kingfisher, glimpsed once
along the Dodder river, vivid
still this grey mid-winter.

It gives birth upon the tide
towards the darkest day.
Near freezing, its cradle

of current barely moving
What you saw this dawn
was only a blown leaf,

some sodden thing
driven sandward, here
onto a ripple of Dublin Bay.

At St. Andrews

for M. C.

I imagine the wild geese
as a series of resolute Vs.
Their wingbeat those first nights

like half-lifted desk lids.
Over the high roofs
of the grim greystone houses

then hingeing south,
the same direction as your bus
each evening to Pittenweem.

The Binder's Notes

It was heavy,
difficult to hold
and as slippery

as that salmon
my son caught
last season.

I lifted it,
like a baby
from its cradle

from trolley to table,
the cockled
creased leaves

spilling over
like an accordion.
The pages open

mid-conversation
between *Aug*.
(St Augustine)

and *Adeo* – in
Latin of course.
The 'M' of *memorit*

seems lit within.
On my report form
I note its condition:

oak-boards
damaged both
front and back;

binding-leather broken;
of five bosses,
one is preserved.

I note the gnawed
edges of vellum,
(a medieval rat!)

and spills
of candle-wax.
But the irreparable

vandalism
of a guide-letter,
crudely excised

is a gaping
silence
which pains me,

like a child's body,
a child of mine,
defiled.

I can only imagine
gold-leaf motifs
of entwined animals

whose tails turn
inexplicably
into serpents,

or vine stems
half hiding
dismayed birds.

If I could effect
a repair
I would, willingly

and gather it
up with
unexpected care.

Colophon

A scholar in the Priory Library
cut right through the calf-skin
of the *Selected Saint Augustine*,
removed 2 of its zoomorphic initials.

Centuries earlier, this one monk
when he'd finished copying
the Latin text – wrote
the following as his end-note:

If anyone deface this book let him die
the death. Let the falling sickness
take him, let him be broken
on the wheel then hanged, Amen.

Dynamo

Why is it that every dream seems *strange*?
And when you write it out it starts to slip,
like the quicksilver, the drops of mercury
our father'd bring home in a small glass tube
from his auto-parts factory workshop.
The mercury'd escape in the blankets
and be lost somewhere in your lap —
or disappear into the furrow of the carpet.
You let it out, that was that. Excitement
always turned to loss. And then on your page
there would be nothing to read, only this:
you know last night I had the strangest dream!

Annaghmakerrig Revisited

You try to make a story of your time
while here – stormhouse your dreams.
The prayer-circle of trees across the lake,
evergreens, willing you to sing. Further
away, gaunt winter ones bundled in ivy,
riding the dromlin: Advent's three kings.
Facing the night outside, the pale, pale light
of a waxing moon, you still can't write.
Reading *Annaghmakerrig* again, its rust-red
machinery beside a broken-down shed,
thistles threaded with spider-mist – as if
those words cast you under their spell.
And nothing can bring back that echoing
aftercall of the grazing Whooper swan.

A Note about the Ninth House

When referring here to *Houses*, we are talking in the language of astrology.

In the Ninth House, that area primarily concerned with systematic understanding and the laws that govern it, there is a reaching out for the meaning of human existence.

Associated with the publishing profession, with philosophical, religious and educational systems, the Ninth House signifies as well, the symbol-making capacity of the psyche – the springs of poetry? A sense of purpose is central to this house; an awarness of patterns; a looking to the future for what is yet to unfold.

It is the House of the traveller, of journeys to far-off places, exploration of the great abroad, but denotes equally, journeys of the mind.

Gail C. Polacsek

About the Author

Photo: Naoise Barry

LOUISE C. CALLAGHAN was born in 1948 and brought up in County Dublin, Ireland. She now lives in Dublin, close to her four children and many grandchildren. Her previous poetry collections are *The Puzzle-Heart* (Salmon, 1999) and *Remember The Birds* (Salmon, 2005). She compiled and edited *Forgotten Light: An Anthology of Memory Poems* (A & A Farmar, 2003). Her poetry, which is widely anthologised in Ireland and England, is included in the *Field Day Anthology: Vols IV & V.* She completed an M.Litt in Creative Writing at St. Andrews University in Scotland (2007) receiving a First Class Honours in her poetry dissertation.